Dubbed by those who knew him as The Old Hero of Gettysburg, John L. Burns
was a civilian who took up his musket and fought for the Union.

THE MARVELS OF STEREOSCOPY

EXPLAINED

* * *

Describing Details of How

Stereoviews Work

And Incidents in Their

Amazing History

The Stereoscopic Album

630 Chestnut St.
Patented October 24, 1871.
W. H. HARDING
Philadelphia.

IN THE LONG-AGO DECADE OF THE 1850S, A MANIA FOR STEREOSCOPY

flourished. Imagine, if you will, that the only images you had of the wide world were what you had seen yourself with your own two eyes. Newspapers and magazines printed only lithographs or engravings; photography was new and novel, a rich man's indulgence; moving picture films had yet to be invented. Then you were offered a stereoscope viewer and your choice of images, from the far-off pyramids of ancient Egypt to the fabled Great Wall of China. Peering through the viewer's lenses, suddenly the wonders of the world were there before you in all their three-dimensional glory. It was as if those sites and the people depicted were alive and breathing there in front of your own two eyes!

Stereoviews were the television or internet of the day. At the peak of their popularity from the 1850s through 1930s, a stereoscope viewer and a carefully chosen collection of stereoviews boasted pride of place in most every middle- and upper-income household around the globe. Stereoviews offered entertainment, education, and armchair travel all in one. They were the virtual reality of their day and age.

The invention of stereoscopy coincided with our comprehension of the concepts of binocular vision and the separate development of photography. In 1838, British scientist Sir Charles Wheatstone presented a paper to the Royal Society demonstrating stereopsis and explaining that we perceive objects in three dimensions because each eye sees a slightly different view; our brains reconcile the two images into one three-dimensional image. Wheatstone unveiled a crude stereoscopic viewer using angled mirrors to look at

Can you afford this?

You can afford this.

drawings. But it wasn't until the 1851 International Exhibition at London's Crystal Palace that everyday people could try out Scottish scientist Sir David Brewster's "improved" binocular stereoscope. Queen Victoria herself proclaimed the stereoscope a marvel of the highest order.

And thus the fad began. From the early 1850s to the late 1930s, millions of stereoscopic images were made by both commercial and amateur photographers. Famous publishers such as Underwood & Underwood, Keystone View Company, B. W. Kilburn, and many more soon began issuing stereoview collections. They documented famous personalities of the times, landmarks around the globe, bible stories brought to life, scientific principles from zoology to astronomy, cycloramas of historical occurrences, and the era's current news events, from the American Civil War and San Francisco's 1868 and 1906 earthquakes to the horrors of World War I. There were even risqué boudoir views available, if you knew who to ask.

Images were on sale at tourist attractions as souvenirs to wow the folk back home. Traveling salesmen carried their cases of wares from door to door, offering viewers and photos to discerning fans eagerly building their collections. Stereoviews provided many people their first photographic views of the world, and they became devoted fans.

By the 1930s, stereoscopy was suddenly old-fashioned and out of fashion. Newspapers now reproduced photographic images, and the new marvels of moving pictures and newsreels brought the world to people in the comfort of theater palaces. The wonders of those once-amazing stereoviews had been surpassed.

But here, in this album of near-forgotten stereoviews, the past lives and breathes once again—in 3D!

⋆ ⋆ ⋆

HOW TO USE THE STEREOSCOPE VIEWER

Relax, and Travel Back in Time!

IN THE EARLY DAYS OF STEREOSCOPY, PHOTOGRAPHERS CREATED the novelty of stereoviews by taking an initial photograph, then moving their camera slightly to a new position to snap the second image. Some inventive photographers soon crafted their own rigs with two, side-by-side cameras. Others used newfangled cameras with dual lenses spaced some 65 millimeters or 2½ inches apart—the distance separating the average person's pupils.

Looking through the lenses of a stereoscope viewer, the human brain recreates the three-dimensional view using the separate views seen with each eye. To do this, all you need do is relax!

To see the stereo image, do not force your eyes to look at the two separate images. Instead, begin by letting your eyes relax, looking above or below the images. Then, slowly move your eyes to the center of the images—and the two images will reappear in 3D. Once you have the images fused together into one, you can move your eyes around to examine different details of the picture and see it in all its depth.

If you wear glasses, try keeping them on while looking through the stereoviewer. The correction in your glasses is often necessary for you to focus on the images. But if it does not work, take off your glasses and try again.

If you're still having difficulties, try moving your head closer or further back from the lenses. You can also tilt your head left or right to adjust the horizontal alignment of the two images.

Simply relax in the comfort of your cozy parlor and prepare to be transported on a journey into the past with your collection of stereoviews and built-in viewer!

General Gettys' House

General James Gettys (1759–1815) founded the town of Gettysburg in 1786, which was then part of his family's farm. Gettys grew up in a log cabin and fought in the American Revolution as a soldier in the Pennsylvania Militia. He purchased from his father 116 acres, the center of which became Gettysburg's town circle. His father owned 386 acres in The Marsh Creek Town Settlement, which was the original name of the hamlet and in 1863 became part of the Gettysburg battlefield.

Gettys built his home near the center of town and married Mary Todd, an ancestor of President Abraham Lincoln's wife. He served as sheriff, town clerk, road builder, tavern owner, state legislator, and a brigadier general of the local militia until his death in 1815. The town he organized became the site of the most famous battle of the Civil War on July 1–3, 1863. Today his monument can be seen in Evergreen Cemetery, which is on Cemetery Hill and remains separate from the nearby national cemetery in Gettysburg National Park. In 1880 his homestead, as pictured, was destroyed by fire.

House of General James Gettys

House of General James Gettys

General Meade's Headquarters

Major General George Gordon Meade never wanted command of the Army of the Potomac. He resented having the responsibility thrust on him by the president on June 28, two days before the Battle of Gettysburg. Like most generals in the Army of the Potomac, Meade preferred fighting defensively instead of aggressively, which is exactly what he did at Gettysburg. At around 3:00 a.m. on July 2 he established headquarters in a small country farmhouse owned by the widow Lydia Leister and her six children. The home lay on the west side of Taneytown Road just behind Cemetery Ridge. The quiet setting, which included apple trees, a picket fence, a flock of chickens, and farm animals, showed no signs of war when Meade entered the building. Unlike some Union commanders, who preferred being farther to the rear, Meade had always been a fighter and wanted to be near the action rather than away from it. Two days later the road serving the home would be scarred with broken fences. Dead horses and mules lying in the pasture beside the road emitted an unpleasant stench that worsened with every day in the sun. Meade and his staff made all the major decisions regarding the Battle of Gettysburg in the Leister homestead.

General Meade's Headquarters

General Meade's Headquarters

Culp's Hill from Cemetery Hill

The topography of 1863 Gettysburg has interesting characteristics not obvious in most stereographs of the area. One of the rare views is the stereograph of Culp's Hill taken from Cemetery Hill. The crest of Culp's Hill is about a half-mile to the east-southeast of Cemetery Hill. Directly south of Cemetery Hill is Cemetery Ridge, and farther to the south are two hills, Little Round Top (650 feet) and Big Round Top (785 feet). There is lower ground and farmland around each topographical feature. The Army of the Potomac occupied this entire network of hills and ridges during the Battle of Gettysburg. Culp's Hill, Little Round Top, and Big Round Top were heavily wooded; Cemetery Hill and Cemetery Ridge were lightly wooded. The Confederate position rested along Seminary Ridge, which was also mostly wooded and about a mile west of Cemetery Ridge. In between were farms and fields.

Militarists described the shape of the Union position as similar to a fishhook, the shank of which stretched from Big Round Top to Cemetery Hill, and then formed a hook by bending around Cemetery Hill to Culp's Hill. Culp's Hill was under constant pressure from the Confederates for three days, and three Union corps became involved defending the position.

Culp's Hill from Cemetery Hill

Culp's Hill from Cemetery Hill

Feeding the Men

It is difficult to know exactly what the African-American cook might have been brewing in the two big kettles hanging over an outdoor makeshift fire. Sometimes soldiers boiled their clothing to get the grit and lice out, and sometimes the same pots were used for cooking. This batch appears to be grub for at least one company of infantry. When fresh beef was available it was often distributed in chunks, sliced into pieces, and cooked with water, peas, potatoes, carrots and other ingredients and served in a slurry resembling a field form of Yankee pot roast. After cooking, the kettles were hauled back to a mess area and ladled out to the company. While on the march, companies often broke into small mess groups, obtained their own rations, and did their own cooking. After African-American cooks began joining the Union Army, they assumed the chore, obtained the rations from the quartermaster, acquired access to all the cooking kettles, pots, pans, and utensils, and began working in teams to feed an entire company at one time, which the cook at the fire is preparing to do.

City Point, Virginia

City Point, Virginia

CRACKER BOXES AND HARDTACK

Every time the Union Army moved, cracker boxes and other provisions went with it. Although the quartermaster department furnished the crackers, known by those who consumed it as hardtack, provost marshal men guarded the boxes. When it became apparent that General Meade, after winning the Battle of Gettysburg, did not intend to pursue Lee's army, boxcars filled with supplies began arriving on the railroad spur serving Gettysburg. Captain J. W. Forsyth of the provost marshal department supervised the company of men sent to safeguard the supplies from being pilfered.

Hardtack had its own history. Known as "Army Bread," the substance was actually a quarter-inch-thick cracker made from unleavened flour. Both sides used hardtack. It was equally unpalatable to both armies and so hard that it had to be softened in water or bacon fat to be eaten. Due to the tooth-breaking nature of the cracker, which often contained grubs, in retrospect it seems odd for the army to have guarded shipments nobody familiar with the contents would ever want to steal.

Aquia Creek, cracker boxes

Aquia Creek, cracker boxes

Railroad Cuts

In 1863, the Gettysburg & Hanover Rail Road served the town from the east but ended on the Taneytown Road, which ran behind Cemetery Hill and terminated in Gettysburg. An extension to the railroad, known as Steven's Projected Railroad, had been partially cut and ran parallel to the Chambersburg Pike, which originated in Gettysburg. Railroad cuts made good cover for military operations because they were banked on both sides. Farther to the west, this particular cut became highly prized by both sides during the first day's battle of Gettysburg. Part of Major General John Buford's dismounted cavalry occupied the cut during the morning to slow down the advance of Henry Heth's Confederates on the Chambersburg Pike. Heth's division eventually pushed the federals out of the cut as reinforcements arrived from Lieutenant General A. P. Hill's III Corps. As Buford slowly withdrew, he directed his batteries covering the Chambersburg Pike to fire into the cut, which again slowed the advance of the enemy. From the outset of the morning battle, Buford's task had been to delay the advance of the enemy, and had he not done so, the Confederates would certainly have secured Cemetery Hill and Cemetery Ridge, the superior defensive position on the battlefield.

Railroad cut going into Gettysburg   *Railroad cut going into Gettysburg*

Attack from the North

This roadway could have been any of four highways leading from the north into Gettysburg; the stereograph gives no clues. Lieutenant General Richard S. Ewell, commanding Lee's II Corps, used those roads to assault Major General Oliver O. Howard's XI Corps on the northern outskirts of Gettysburg at 2:30 p.m. on July 1, 1863. Because most of the Army of the Potomac had not yet reached Gettysburg, Howard took overall command of the battlefield and for several hours fought A. P. Hill's corps on the right and Ewell's corps on his front. Forced to fall back, Howard continued to block Ewell's advance on the roads north of Gettysburg until reinforcements arrived. He then fell back through town and secured a lodgment on Cemetery Hill, which Major General George Gordon Meade, commanding the Army of the Potomac, had occupied with fresh forces and for defense. The delaying actions by the I and XI Army Corps against superior strength produced battlefield advantages for the Army of the Potomac, leaving Lee with the lower ground and a lengthier defensive position along Seminary Ridge.

Battlefield of Gettysburg, northern portion

Battlefield of Gettysburg, northern portion

Lutheran Theological Seminary

The Lutheran Theological Seminary sits on the northern end of Seminary Hill about a half mile east of the outskirts of 1863 Gettysburg. Founded in 1826, it is America's oldest Lutheran seminary. From the cupola atop the building one can look down the Chambersburg Pike, which is what Major Buford did on July 1, 1863, when he observed Confederates camped at Cashtown marching toward Gettysburg. When Union forces later withdrew to Cemetery Hill, General Lee and his staff used the seminary's cupola as their observation post. The building, as well as adjacent homes for professors and theology students, became a temporary field hospital and continued as such for several weeks after the battle. As patients began to heal, they were moved to the Camp Letterman military hospital created in Gettysburg. A new seminary was built after the war, and the old seminary pictured in the stereograph now houses the Adams County Historical Society. Scattered throughout the grounds are markers related to the battle, as well as several scattered pieces of artillery representing the approximate location of batteries during the battles.

Gettysburg Theological Seminary

Gettysburg Theological Seminary

View from Seminary Hill

The Gettysburg observatory did not exist at the time this scene of the battlefield was photographed. Instead, Major General John Buford used the cupola on top of the Lutheran seminary when the first Confederate patrols appeared on the Chambersburg Pike on June 30, 1863. No action followed. The Confederates observed a few Union cavalry patrolling Gettysburg and returned to Cashtown to report their observations to Lieutenant General A. P. Hill, commanding the Army of Northern Virginia's III Corps. They also informed Hill that a large shipment of shoes had recently been received at Gettysburg.

Buford reported the presence of Confederate patrols to Major General John Reynolds, who arrived on the morning of July 1 and joined Buford in the Lutheran cupola on Seminary Hill. It was from there the two Union commanders could see the landscape of what became the first day's opening battle of Gettysburg. They also observed Brigadier General James J. Pettigrew's brigade from Henry Heth's division approaching the town along the Chambersburg Pike. Buford recognized the importance of Gettysburg and organized his badly outnumbered cavalry to slow the Confederate advance. Reynolds immediately ordered up his I Corps, which set the stage for the three-day battle that followed.

Battlefield from Observatory   *Battlefield from Observatory*

Lee's Headquarters

On the afternoon of July 1, 1863, General Robert E. Lee moved into an old stone home owned by Congressman Thaddeus Stevens but occupied by Mrs. Mary Thompson, known locally as The Widow Thompson. At the time the home may have been a duplex, with Mrs. Thompson occupying one side while Lee and his staff occupied the other. The home suited Lee's purpose because it was located on the Chambersburg Pike and connected to several other roads used by his army. His headquarters was also located near the center of his battle line, which stretched down Seminary Ridge on one side and to Culp's Hill on the other side. The Widow Thompson did not like the Rebels, but she admitted that while "the gentlemanly deportment of General Lee whilst in her house" made a favorable impression, she complained bitterly "of the robbery and general destruction of her goods by some of the attendants."

The home reopened in 1922 as the Lee Museum, displaying artifacts found on the battlefield. Since that time it has been in continuous operation and remains one of the oldest museums in Gettysburg.

General Lee's Headquarters

General Lee's Headquarters

GUNS ON CULP'S HILL

There was never a day during the three days of Gettysburg that the Confederates did not try to seize Culp's Hill. Their best opportunity occurred on July 1 when Lieutenant General Richard S. Ewell's II Corps entered Gettysburg from the north and pushed Oliver O. Howard's XI Corps through the town. Jubal A. Early's division was in good position to move down the west bank of Rock Creek and attack either Cemetery Hill or Culp's Hill, but Ewell failed to order it done. Instead, the Confederates spent the next two days battering against the defenses on Culp's Hill in a futile attempt to drive off the federals. The army howitzer in the stereograph faces slightly to the north and looks out across the battlefield of Culp's Hill, which is rich with fields of hay and summer crops.

Guns on Culp's Hill

Guns on Culp's Hill

DEFENDING THE HILLS

When Major General Oliver O. Howard withdrew from Gettysburg on the afternoon of July 1, he put his XI Corps on Cemetery Hill. Two of his divisions, one commanded by Carl Schurz and the other by Adolph von Steinwehr, immediately began improving the defenses on the left flank of the hill, part of which was mostly open ground and the rest wooded. The row of abatis shown in the stereograph was part of the defensive works in the woods that ran along the Taneytown and Emmitsburg Road on the west slope of Cemetery Hill. The only two attacks on Cemetery Hill occurred on the north slope on July 2, both of which were repulsed. Being so close to Culp's Hill on the left, Cemetery Hill naturally attracted the enemy's attention, but both hills were adjacent to and in supporting distance of each other with artillery in between. Any attack on the east slope of Cemetery Hill or the west slope of Culp's Hill would draw enfilading fire from the other hill. For this reason, all the heavy Confederate attacks on Culp's Hill occurred on the far side.

Breastworks on the left wing

Breastworks on the left wing

George Sykes and Staff

Major General George Sykes (center) had fought in every major battle of the Army of the Potomac since the beginning of the war. Unlike most generals, who led volunteers, Sykes commanded veterans from the regular army. After the Battle of Chancellorsville on May 1–4, 1863, he brought his division to Maryland a few days before the Battle of Gettysburg. On June 28, when Major General George Gordon Meade took command of the Army of the Potomac, Sykes assumed command of Meade's V Corps and placed it in a defensive position near Pipe Creek, Maryland. On that day he sat with his staff and began studying maps showing roads leading into Pennsylvania.

After arriving on Cemetery Hill late on July 1, Sykes V Corps became involved in one of the most critical battles fought at Gettysburg during the following afternoon. His men valiantly rescued the Union left flank after two Confederate divisions had crushed the III Corps. Sykes then secured Little Round Top, thus preventing General Lee's Confederates from flanking the Union army off Cemetery Ridge and gaining the best tactical position on the battlefield.

General George Sykes and Staff

General George Sykes and Staff

General Hunt's Guns

Brigadier General Henry J. Hunt, commanding the Reserve Artillery for the Army of the Potomac, began moving his guns down the Baltimore Pike during the afternoon of July 1 and arrived on Cemetery Ridge late that night. The line of march at times stretched for a mile, raising dust as the wheels of artillery carriages and wagons bumped over rough roads. Hundreds of horses strained on their harnesses and mules under their packs added their complaints in a cacophony of constant noise. Shown are light artillery pieces, while farther to the rear the heavy cannon followed. Most of the guns in the stereograph are 3-inch field pieces, some with smooth bores and some rifled, but Hunt's command also carried 6- and 12-pounders and a few 24- and 32-pound howitzers. All these guns would play a prominent role mowing down "Pickett's Charge" on July 3, 1863, in the final battle of Gettysburg. General Hunt and his guns played a major role in all the battles of the Army of the Potomac, but nowhere would they have a more devastating impact than at Gettysburg. In this image, Union artillery amass at Fair Oaks, Virginia.

Fair Oaks, Gibson's batteries

Fair Oaks, Gibson's batteries

The U.S. Sanitary Commission

The Gettysburg battle erupted so suddenly on July 1 that attending to the wounded fell entirely on regimental surgeons and their small staffs. Not until the smoke of battle cleared and Confederates withdrew did the first members of the U.S. Sanitary Commission arrive. The stereograph shows the men and women of the commission attired in their best Sunday clothes for a group picture outside a home serving as a hospital. The volunteers played an important role during the war by raising hygienic standards in the camps, improving care for the wounded, sending food and medical supplies to the injured to ensure their proper diet and care, and preparing a directory of the sick and wounded in army field and central hospitals so relatives and friends could visit or send packages. For injured soldiers who were well enough to travel home, the commission maintained lodges near railroad stations where men too weak to travel all the way could stay and rest. Although the Sanitary Commission when first formed drew skeptics, the men and women involved took their work seriously and saved uncountable lives.

Fredericksburg, Sanitary Commission

Fredericksburg, Sanitary Commission

Alfred R. Waud: Sketching the War

Alfred Rodoph Waud, an Englishman born in 1828, migrated to the United States in 1850 and began working as an illustrator for periodicals and books until the outbreak of the Civil War. He joined the staff of the New York Illustrated News as a field artist and soon became known for his sketches of army and navy life. Traveling on horseback with pencil and sketchbook, he reported the war from First Bull Run to the final surrender at Appomattox Court House. While working for the *Illustrated News*, he converted many of his sketches into woodcuts to facilitate the printing process.

In 1862 Waud joined *Harper's Weekly* and remained one of the most popular and prolific artists of the war. He followed the Army of the Potomac in all of its campaigns, which brought him to Gettysburg in July 1863. Unlike photographers who waited in the rear for the action to end, Waud went into battle with the army, occupied an exposed position in plain view, and worked on sketches as bullets whizzed by his ears. While many illustrators of the day made sketches from photographs, Waud would take a seat on a rock and make his drawings in the smoke of battle.

Gettysburg, Alfred R. Waud

Gettysburg, Alfred R. Waud

Confederate Dead in McPherson's Woods

The first day's Battle of Gettysburg on July 1, 1863, can best be described as a skirmish that rapidly escalated into a full-blown battle. Neither army was in place, and the two sides converged on the town from different directions. The battle began slowly when A. P. Hill sent Henry Heth's division toward Gettysburg to capture a supply of shoes reported there. Major General John Buford's cavalry division happened to be in Gettysburg on a reconnaissance for the Army of the Potomac when pickets reported a large Confederate column on the Chambersburg Pike, which went through Cashtown. Buford dismounted his cavalry and sent skirmishers ahead to check the enemy's advance. He also brought up his horse artillery and placed the guns on both sides of the road.

After the fighting began, Hill pushed forward William Dorsey Pender's division, which fell in behind Heth and spread along both sides of the pike. The Confederates had the advantage in men, but Buford's dismounted cavalry carried seven-shot Spencer repeating rifles. The battle moved on to McPherson's Ridge, a slender hill southwest of Gettysburg, where fighting intensified as more units arrived on the field. By early afternoon McPherson's Woods were littered with the dead and wounded. The stereograph shows where a Confederate unit charged from the woods and fell on the grassy pasture nearby.

Gettysburg - Confederate dead

Gettysburg - Confederate dead

Union Dead East of McPherson's Ridge

The Confederates were not the only soldiers to die on the first day of battle at Gettysburg. McPherson's Ridge can be seen in the distance, where it gradually slopes toward Willoughby Run where another fight ensued. At 10:30 a.m. federal infantry from Abner Doubleday's division began arriving from the Emmitsburg Road. Major General John F. Reynolds, commanding the I Corps, was already there and double-quicked Doubleday's men across the fields and into position below McPherson's Ridge. Reynolds got too close to the fighting and lost his life positioning his men. By then, the Confederates had built up superior strength, charged out of the woods, and began pushing for Seminary Ridge. Around noon the fighting subsided while both sides reorganized for another attack. By then, the field below McPherson's Ridge was already littered with the dead. A photographer circulating through the battlefield a few days later discovered the bloated corpses of several Union solders lying together in a meadow east of McPherson's Ridge.

Union dead, first day　　　　　　　　　　　　*Union dead, first day*

John L. Burns: Local Hero

The home of John L. Burns on Chambersburg Street in Gettysburg would probably have gone unnoticed by historians had the owner not come off his porch on July 1, 1863, to fight for the Union. The stereograph, taken from the distance by Matthew Brady's photographer Timothy H. O'Sullivan, is similar to the latter's close-up showing Burns with crutches, which he needed while convalescing from his wounds, and his flintlock musket, which he no longer needed because the enemy had fled.

   The story of Burns' heroism eventually expanded to legendary proportions, giving him a place in histories written about the Battle of Gettysburg. When his large home was razed after his death, veterans thought something should be done to recognize his services. This led to legislation providing funds for a monument, which on July 1, 1903, was placed between the 7th Wisconsin and 150th Pennsylvania monuments at McPherson's Ridge. By then John Burns had become a national icon. Sculptor Albert G. Bureau depicted Burns as a defiant veteran who hated Rebels, and who, with a clenched fist, valiantly carried his flintlock musket into battle. Today, on a boulder lugged from the old battlefield, stands the six-foot, one-inch bronze statue of the "old hero of Gettysburg."

Home of John L. Burns

Home of John L. Burns

Breastworks on Culp's Hill

On the Union right flank, curling about and resembling the business end of a fishhook, stood Culp's Hill, which was separated by a few hundred yards from the base of Cemetery Hill. Meade understood the importance of protecting his right flank, and when Major General Oliver O. Howard retreated from Gettysburg on July 1, he occupied Cemetery Hill. When Major General Henry W. Slocum arrived with the XII Corps, he occupied Culp's Hill. On July 2 General Lee decided to attack Culp's Hill with Ewell's Corps while General Longstreet attacked the Union left flank near the Round Tops, which were located at the opposite end of the Union defensive line that stretched across Cemetery Ridge. Slocum's men occupied the heights on Culp's Hill and threw up breastworks on the slope. Breastworks were hastily constructed temporary fortifications mostly composed of earth, logs, limbs, and rocks. They were high enough for a soldier to stand, fire, reload, and still feel somewhat protected. Scores of breastworks like the one pictured dotted the slope of Culp's Hill, enabling Slocum's men to repulse several attempts by the enemy to capture the position.

Paintings such as this were popular stereoscopic views when published after the Civil War.

Battlefield breastworks on Culp's Hill

Battlefield breastworks on Culp's Hill

Shot and Shell Devastates the Round Tops

The thickest woods on the Gettysburg battlefield grew on Little Round Top, a 650-foot hill, and Big Round Top, a 785-foot hill. On the afternoon of July 2, Major General John Bell Hood's artillery opened on Little Round to drive away Union pickets as 500 men from the 15th Alabama began scaling Big Round Top. Major General Gouverneur K. Warren heard artillery fire above the noise of battle in his front and observed Confederates forming to breach the Union left flank. He dispatched Colonel Strong Vincent's brigade, which he found in reserve, to defend Little Round Top. Vincent suffered a mortal wound stopping the Confederate attack, and two of his regimental commanders were killed that day.

Days later, photographers and artists stomped through the area to witness the wreckage caused by the defense of the Round Tops. The bodies had been removed, but the effect of shot and shell showed on the scarred landscape east of Plum Run and near the Devil's Den. Trees had been snapped in half and others were uprooted by repeated strikes from artillery shells. Even the boulders, so common to the area, showed scars from ricocheting shrapnel and airborne debris.

Battlefield effect of shot and shell

Battlefield effect of shot and shell

Sickles' Salient

During the morning of July 2, General Meade spread the Army of the Potomac along Cemetery Ridge with each corps connected on its flanks by another corps. Meade wanted to fight a defensive battle and waited for Lee to attack. Instead of connecting his right flank to General Hancock's left flank, Major General Daniel E. Sickles moved his III Corps forward. This created "Sickles' Salient," which brought about the battle in the Wheat Field and at Trostle's farm with Lieutenant General James Longstreet's divisions from the Confederate I Corps. What started as a moderate exchange of rifle fire between skirmishes erupted into a full-scale struggle at 4:00 p.m. The fight rapidly spread to the Peach Orchard, the Devil's Den, and Little Round Top. Meade began rushing reinforcements into Sickles' Salient to shore up the left flank. In the confusion on the battlefield, an officer on horseback shouted orders as his men scurried forward into the smoke of artillery and rifle fire, in a scene typical of many engagements fought at Gettysburg. Sickles eventually fell back to Cemetery Ridge, and when A. P. Hill's corps failed to attack the Union center, Longstreet also fell back, leaving thousands of casualties on the battlefield.

Battle of Gettysburg

Battle of Gettysburg

Battle of the Peach Orchard

After moving to his assigned sector on Cemetery Ridge, Major General Daniel E. Sickles moved his III Corps forward, without permission, to occupy higher ground in front of Meade's battle line. This resulted in the formation of "Sickles' Salient," which brought on the battle of the Peach Orchard when at 4:00 p.m. Confederates began shifting toward the Round Tops. When Lieutenant General James Longstreet found Sickles' Salient in the way, Confederate brigades began closing in from the right, first on the Wheat Field and then on the Peach Orchard, which lay far in advance of what General Meade had established as his defensive position. Sickles' brigades became enfiladed by fire from the left, forcing Meade to push forward reinforcements to stop each brigade-sized counterattack launched by the Confederates. Without help from four army corps posted on Cemetery Ridge, Sickles' brigades in the Peach Orchard and the Wheat Field faced annihilation or surrender because of their exposed and extended position. The stereograph shows men being rushed into position at the Peach Orchard while their officers on horseback directed the movement that eventually allowed Sickles' corps to return to Cemetery Ridge, but not before suffering enormous casualties.

Battle of the Peach Orchard

Battle of the Peach Orchard

Little Round Top

To an observer on the field, Little Round Top looked no different than any other nondescript minor hill one might see on the edge of any Pennsylvania farm. At 4:00 p.m. on July 2, it quickly became central to the control of Cemetery Ridge when three Confederate brigades tried to turn the left flank of the Army of the Potomac. There were no federal forces on Little Round Top but a few pickets, whose orders were to fire a few shots if attacked and retire. The firing immediately alerted General Warren, who detached Colonel Strong Vincent's brigade of four regiments from the 1st Division, V Corps, and ordered it to hold the hill at all costs. Vincent led the brigade across the crest and positioned it on the southern slope facing the enemy and posted the 20th Maine on the far left followed by the 83rd Pennsylvania, 44th New York, and the 16th Michigan. Two Confederate brigades under the command of Jerome Robertson and Evander M. Law were repulsed on Vincent's right flank and William C. Oates's 15th Alabama was driven from the field by a bayonet charge by the 20th Maine, which had depleted its ammunition. Casualties among the Confederates were especially heavy, but Vincent lost his life while rallying his men. On the evening of July 2 General Meade immediately requested Vincent's promotion to brigadier general, but the colonel died four days later unaware of his promotion.

Little Round Top

Little Round Top

Dead Confederate Sharpshooter at Little Round Top

In early July the fields surrounding Gettysburg were rich with ripening summer crops, but there were hilly sections filled with rocky outcroppings that made excellent cover for sharpshooters. This dead Confederate fell during the second day's battle, July 2, during the fight for the possession of Little Round Top. After severe fighting ended in the Wheat Field, the Peach Orchard, and the Apple Orchard, where the Union III Corps suffered severe casualties, Confederate sharpshooters in greater numbers began drifting to the right around 4:00 p.m. to assault two hills known as Little Round Top and Big Round Top, which at the time were guarded by a handful of pickets. As more federal troops rushed to Little Round Top, a furious fight erupted for possession of the hill, which actually had been neglected by General Meade although it protected the Army of the Potomac's left flank. Hundreds of men were killed during the afternoon, including several generals and the lone Confederate sharpshooter whose body remained unattended beneath the rocks where he died.

Confederate sharpshooter

Confederate sharpshooter

Carnage at Trostle's Farm

Major General Daniel E. Sickles, commanding the Army of the Potomac III Corps, used Abraham Trostle's house and barn as his headquarters. Instead of being on Cemetery Ridge with the rest of army, Sickles chose different ground after a dispute with General Meade. This created a salient with poorly protected flanks and attracted the attention of the enemy. One feature of the area was Trostle's Lane, which ran north, connected Cemetery Ridge with the Emmitsburg Road, and facilitated the movement of men and artillery. During a late afternoon attack on July 2 by Longstreet's corps, the battle in the Wheat Field and the Peach Orchard gradually expanded, encompassing Trostle's farm. Union troops retreated in the direction of the house, drawing artillery fire that struck the house and killed most of the horses in the barnyard. During the bombardment a shell fragment struck Sickles' right leg, which he later lost along with his reputation for disobeying Meade's orders. An ambulance hauled Sickles away in the midst of wild confusion and bitter fighting. Timothy H. O'Sullivan's stereograph of the dead horses lying in Trostle's barnyard provides a vivid image of the shelling and fighting that occurred at Sickles' misplaced headquarters.

Fight at Trostle's Farm

Fight at Trostle's Farm

Fight at Spangler's Spring

Spangler's Spring was located below the southeastern base of Culp's Hill, and during the night of July 2 there was an alleged truce between certain Confederate and Union elements who shared the spring's cool waters. The story has never been verified, but it is certain that the following day the bluecoats and graycoats faced off and slaughtered each other. During the night, Major General Henry W. Slocum's XII Corps reoccupied the vital crest of Culp's Hill, and around 4:00 a.m. on July 3 Major General Edward Johnson sent five Confederate brigades up the hill to take the crest. For seven hours the fighting raged as Confederates tried unsuccessfully to force their way through rows of heavily defended federal abatis. The firing became so intense that it destroyed one of the area's finest oak forests and knocked to pieces the town's favorite picnic ground. Johnson tried three times, twice with frontal assaults and once with a flank attack, all of which failed to dislodge the federals. The Confederates collected most of their wounded and withdrew before noon. The stereograph, though taken at Spangler's Spring, depicted a scene quite different from the killing that took place a few hundred yards away on Culp's Hill.

Fight at Spangler Spring

Fight at Spangler Spring

Merwin and the Battle of the Wheat Field

The marker inscribed "here lies . . . Merwin" does not leave many clues, but on July 2, 1863, Lieutenant Colonel Henry C. Merwin led the 27th Connecticut Infantry Regiment into the battle of the Wheat Field. He was part of John R. Brooke's brigade from John C. Caldwell's II Corps division. Caldwell sent the brigade into the Wheat Field to reinforce Sickles' corps, which had run into a mincing machine from Longstreet's divisions. Brooke ordered the brigade to "Fix bayonets," which was equivalent to ordering a suicide assault. The attack, however, worked. Brooke's brigade, aided by the 148th Pennsylvania on its left and two Union brigades on its left pushed the Confederates across Plum Run's ravine and to the western edge of Rose's Woods near the Wheat Field. The assault was also costly. Merwin lost his life, and Colonel Hiram Brown of the 145th Pennsylvania fell with a serious wound. Members of the 27th Connecticut eventually raised funds for a marker and returned after the war to place it where Merwin fell.

Here Lies Merwin

Here Lies Merwin

Little Round Top Monument

What the photographer described as the Little Round Top Monument is actually the monolithic structure erected to memorialize the 91st Pennsylvania Infantry Regiment, which Brigadier General Stephen H. Weed hurriedly led to the defense of the hill during the afternoon of July 2, 1863. The real credit for the defense of Little Round Top belongs to the forces under the command of Colonel Strong Vincent, whose brigade consisted of the 20th Maine, 83rd Pennsylvania, 44th New York, and 16th Michigan. The 20th Maine held the extreme left flank of Vincent's battle line and there is a monument on Little Round Top to mark the spot. The 16th Michigan occupied the extreme right of the line where its monument now stands on Little Round Top. The 83rd Pennsylvania's monument is on Sykes Avenue and near but not in its proper 1863 position next to the 20th Maine's right flank. Atop this monument is the statue of Strong Vincent. The largest and most expensive monument and next in line on Sykes Avenue is the massive granite castle honoring the officers and men of the 44th New York. Farther north on Sykes Avenue is the portrait statue of Major General Gouverneur Warren, who is credited with rushing Vincent's brigade to Little Round Top to stop the Confederates from flanking the Army of the Potomac on Cemetery Ridge. Both Weed and Vincent died in the defense of Little Round Top.

Little Round Top Monument

Little Round Top Monument

Dead at Little Round Top

The sharp fight at Little Round Top left the ground strewn with corpses. Of the four regiments from Strong Vincent's brigade that went into battle on the afternoon of July 2, 1863, six officers and eighty-two enlisted men were killed on the hill. Another seventeen officers and 236 enlisted men suffered wounds. Eleven enlisted men completely disappeared and were either captured or mutilated beyond recognition. The aggregate casualties totaled 352 officers and men.

An accurate count could never be made of Confederate casualties, which were only known to be much heavier. The base of the left slope of Little Round Top became known as the Slaughter Pen because dead Confederates lay strewn among the rocks with some draped over their comrades. During the final charge of the 20th Maine, 101 Confederates surrendered. It took days to remove the dead from the Slaughter Pen and the nearby Devil's Den, which gave newspaper photographers and sightseers time to hike along the base of Little Round Top to look at the carnage and take pictures of the grisly scenes after the Confederates withdrew.

Dead at Little Round Top

Dead at Little Round Top

General Pleasonton

The Union cavalry, which had not been able to compete with the Confederate cavalry, came into its own during the Gettysburg campaign. Major General Alfred Pleasonton took command of the Army of the Potomac's Cavalry Corps on May 22, 1863, and on June 9 attacked and nearly defeated Jeb Stuart's vaunted Confederate cavalry at Brandy Station. The action became the forerunner to the Gettysburg campaign. During Lee's march into Pennsylvania, Pleasonton harassed the Confederate cavalry, pressed it hard, and prevented Stuart from meaningfully assisting Lee during the battle of Gettysburg. Stuart did not reach Gettysburg until the afternoon of July 2. When later that day Lee sent Stuart to cut Meade's line of communications on the Baltimore Pike, Pleasonton sent three cavalry brigades to stop the raid. Both sides fought mounted and on foot, and after being heavily engaged Stuart fell back without accomplishing his mission. On the following day one of Pleasonton's cavalry division commanders recklessly attacked a Confederate infantry brigade and paid a heavy price. Pleasonton escaped responsibility for the irresponsible attack, partly because of the fine work done by his cavalry prior to the poorly conceived action.

General Alfred Pleasonton

General Alfred Pleasonton

Guns and Gun Crews

On July 2, Major General Winfield Scott Hancock, commanding the II Corps, held the center position on Cemetery Ridge. Early in the morning he began moving his artillery into a commanding position overlooking the fields between his position and the Confederates holding Seminary Ridge. By then the heavier 32-pounder field guns had been brought up, aligned a short distance behind the front line, and bracketed in on the enemy position with shells and other ammunition accessible nearby.

Hancock's artillery had a busy day because the Confederates attacked the Union left in the Peach Orchard, the Wheat Field, and the Devil's Den, and the right at Culp's Hill. The Confederate attacks were poorly co-ordinated, making it possible for each piece of artillery to be turned to sweep the fields over which the enemy attacked. The Confederates were repulsed at both ends of the battlefield, but Hancock suffered a wound and turned the command over to Brigadier General John Gibbon, a career artillerist, who made the necessary adjustments as the army prepared for the third day's battle.

Guns and gun crews

Guns and gun crews

Devil's Den

Every major Civil War battle had its Slaughter Pen, Bloody Angle, Hornet's Nest, or some other suitable name capable of conjuring up visions of death and wholesale blood-spilling. Gettysburg had its Devil's Den, which was a demonic mass of huge rocks occupying the lower reaches of Little Round Top, which, on July 2, represented part of the exposed left flank of the Army of the Potomac. Some of the boulders were the size of a small house. When the Confederates attacked at 4:00 p.m., the boulders of the Devil's Den were defended by Brigadier General J. H. Hobart Ward's brigade and a six-gun battery. Struck on the front and flanks, Ward's brigade fought a stubborn battle for ninety minutes until overwhelmed by regiments from Texas and Georgia. One of Ward's regiments lost half its men in twenty-five minutes, but the determined Confederates suffered severe losses gaining a position they held until Lee's withdrawal two days later. The Confederates left behind at least one of their comrades among the lonely rocks, a scene a photographer prowling the battlefield captured several days later.

Dead man in the Devil's Den

Dead man in the Devil's Den

Hancock's Troops

Major General Winfield Scott Hancock recognized the natural strength of Cemetery Ridge as well as the importance of placing troops on Culp's Hill to protect the federal right flank, and it was his recommendations to General Meade that provided the Army of the Potomac with the best defensive position on the battlefield. Hancock placed his corps in the central position on Cemetery Ridge, knowing the men could be moved to the right or the left if Lee attacked the flanks. Looking west from Cemetery Ridge, Hancock could see Seminary Ridge in the distance, about a mile away. In between lay undulating farmland with the Bliss House to the right and the Codori House to the left, which the photographer omitted. The federal position formed the shape of a fishhook with the shank running from the Round Tops on the south to Culp's Hill on the north, which from above resembled the hook's barb. Hancock's division occupied part of the shank that ran along Cemetery Ridge. Most of the fighting on July 2 took place on the flanks, but on July 3 during Pickett's Charge, Hancock's II Corps bore the brunt of the attack and repulsed the Confederates over the ground in the photograph during the final battle of Gettysburg.

Position of Hancock's Troops

Position of Hancock's Troops

Rock Creek, Near Culp's Hill

Rock Creek flows south, passing a short distance from the eastern base of Culp's Hill, which protected the right flank of the Army of the Potomac. Lieutenant General Richard S. Ewell's II Corps tried twice to push Major General Henry W. Slocum's XII Corps off the hill so Confederate artillery could be brought to the summit and enfilade the Army of the Potomac on Cemetery Hill. The result would have been devastating had Slocum's corps not remained steadfast. At 6:00 p.m. on July 2, after softening Slocum's defenders with artillery fire, Ewell sent three divisions forward in a disconnected attack that succeeded in getting a foothold on the hill where federal strength had been reduced to strengthen Sickles and other units on the far left. By nightfall the assault ended, and the Confederates fell back to regroup. On July 3, while Lee prepared to attack Meade's center, the Confederates made one more attempt to capture Culp's Hill. While part of Ewell's force assaulted the hill from Rock Creek, a second force attempted to assault Cemetery Hill. Slocum's division, now reinforced by the I Corps, repulsed the attack on Culp's Hill and by 10:30 a.m. had driven the Confederates back to Rock Creek with severe casualties, thus ending the fighting on Meade's right flank.

Rock Creek, below Culp's Hill

Rock Creek, below Culp's Hill

Charge of the 2nd Massachusetts

In the early morning of July 3, due to a misinterpreted order from Major General Henry W. Slocum, a courier from headquarters sent Lieutenant Colonel Charles R. Mudge's 2nd Massachusetts and Lieutenant Colonel John R. Fessler's 27th Indiana into a gallant but hopeless charge against three Confederate brigades formed around the base of Culp's Hill. The messenger never understood the order, delivered it orally, and in the transmission completely garbled it. "Are you sure that is the order?" asked Mudge. "Yes," the courier replied. "Well," said Mudge, "it is murder, but it's the order."

The courier said there must be no delay, so Mudge formed the regiment along a rail fence, faced the men toward a woods heavily defended by the enemy, and shouted, "Up men, over the works! Forward, double quick!" The regiment gave a Yankee cheer, sprang over the fence, and charged across the meadow as fast as good order and soggy ground allowed. The 27th Indiana also advanced but had to first change front because it faced Rock Creek, leaving the 2nd Massachusetts in the meadow without support. From behind rocks the Confederates opened with a blaze of rifle fire. In less than five minutes the 2nd Massachusetts lost Mudge, four color bearers, and 250 men.

Meadow of the 2nd Massachussetts charge

Meadow of the 2nd Massachussetts charge

CHARGE OF THE 147TH PENNSYLVANIA

Around mid-morning on July 3, Major General Edward Johnson twice sent his Confederate brigades forward in an effort to seize Culp's Hill and draw federal reinforcements away from a section on Cemetery Ridge that General Lee intended to attack later in the day in what became known as "Pickett's Charge." After being repulsed twice, Johnson tried once more by assaulting across an open field near Spangler's Spring. In the woods across the field waited 600 federals from the 147th Pennsylvania and the 5th Ohio. They had been there most of the morning holding the right flank of General Wadsworth's I Corps on Culp's Hill. The woods formed a saddle between Culp's Hill and a smaller hill, and the ground was marshy with lots of underbrush and scattered boulders.

The Confederates attacked at double-quick but were slowed by wet ground. Soldiers of the 147th Pennsylvania held their fire and opened with the 5th Ohio at one hundred yards. Confederates fell but still came forward, their files decimated by the firing of the two federal regiments in the woods. As the Rebel lines staggered backwards, finally breaking and stumbling back across the open field, the 147th Pennsylvania charged out of the woods but found nothing in their front but the bodies of the fallen enemy.

Woods where the 147th Pennsylvania charged

Woods where the 147th Pennsylvania charged

The New York Batteries and the "Bloody Angle"

At 1:45 p.m. on July 3, 1863, following a heavy artillery preparation, more than 13,000 Confederates came from the woods on Seminary Ridge, crossed a half mile of open field, and began ascending the slope of Cemetery Ridge in the final assault at Gettysburg known as "Pickett's Charge." Brigadier General Henry J. Hunt, commanding the Union artillery, anticipated the assault and brought his guns forward and placed them on the crest of Cemetery Ridge overlooking the Emmitsburg Road. The federal infantry waited behind breastworks and stone walls, watching as Hunt's artillery opened gaps in Pickett's line with shells of all sizes. By the time the Confederates formed to assault the crest, Hunt's artillery had punched huge holes in the quarter-mile-wide enemy line. Then began the final assault on a position known only as the "little clump of trees" at the "Bloody Angle."

Although the Confederate advance began in good order, canister and grapeshot tore the enemy lines to pieces. Soldiers hesitated and many fell back. The New York batteries pictured in the stereograph participated in the battle, fighting alongside U.S. batteries manned by regulars. As Pickett's men advanced, fighting intensified at Bloody Angle. Lieutenant Alonzo Cushing, appointed to West Point from New York, had already been wounded three times when he rolled a gun down to the stone wall and died directing its fire at point-blank range at a handful of Confederates breaking into the Angle. Historians called it "the high tide of the Confederacy" as the enemy withdrew to Seminary Ridge. Lee retreated the following evening and took his battle-scarred army back to Virginia.

First New York Battery

First New York Battery

Custer Takes an Old Acquaintance Prisoner

The Civil War made George Armstrong Custer (right) famous. From First Bull Run to Lee's surrender at Appomattox, Custer participated in every battle of the Army of the Potomac but one. After the cavalry fight at Brandy Station on June 9, 1863, Custer took command of the 2nd Brigade, 3rd Cavalry Division, known as the Michigan Brigade. During the many cavalry fights that took place in the days before the Battle of Gettysburg, Custer distinguished himself and on one occasion captured Lieutenant James B. Washington (left), an old acquaintance from the pre-war years on the frontier.

One of the gravest problems General Lee encountered at Gettysburg was the absence of his cavalry, which had been delayed by a cavalry fight at Hanover, Pennsylvania, in which Custer participated. As a consequence, the Confederate cavalry never reached Gettysburg until late on July 2. When Lee sent his cavalry around the Union right on July 3, Custer clashed again with the southern sabers and sent them reeling back to their own lines. There is no record of what became of Lieutenant Washington, but Custer lost his life on June 25, 1876, while fighting a superior force of Sioux Indians at Little Big Horn, Montana territory.

James B. Washington and George A. Custer

James B. Washington and George A. Custer

Gettysburg National Cemetery

The Gettysburg National Cemetery was dedicated on November 19, 1863, four months and sixteen days after the last day of battle. It is located on Cemetery Hill, where part of the Army of the Potomac made its stand. The stereograph shows the entrance to the national cemetery, but in the background stands the tall and exquisite Soldiers' National Monument, which was sculpted by Randolph Rogers and erected at the center of the cemetery on July 1, 1869. With the support of Pennsylvania governor Andrew Curtin, the tract was purchased from local landowners to provide a common resting place for Union dead. Some 3,512 bodies were disinterred from shallow and inadequate graves throughout the battlefield and by March 1864 had been reburied in the cemetery. Of that number, the names of 979 remain unknown. Removal of Confederate dead from field burial plots did not occur until 1870, when the first of 3,320 bodies were exhumed and sent to final resting places in the South.

The main speaker at the dedication ceremony was distinguished orator Edward Everett, who talked for more than two hours about the Battle of Gettysburg. Abraham Lincoln then spoke for two minutes, delivering what later became his famous Gettysburg Address. Nobody thought much of Lincoln's speech until they read it in the newspapers. Even Edward Everett later admitted he had been outdone, admitting that Lincoln had expressed the meaning of the occasion better in two minutes than he had in two hours.

Gettysburg National Cemetery

Gettysburg National Cemetery

Soldiers National Monument

The Soldiers' National Monument shown in the distance is approximately where President Lincoln delivered the Gettysburg Address, but the monument was not commissioned until the summer of 1869. The rows of graves, however, were already in place, and more were being added every day. The complex, originally called the Soldiers' National Cemetery at Gettysburg, became a national cemetery on May 1, 1872, when control was transferred to the War Department. Over the years the cemetery became a burial ground for soldiers who fought in other wars. Currently administered by the National Park Service, the cemetery contains the remains of more than 6,000 soldiers dating back to the Mexican-American War.

Cemetery Hill still has two distinct cemeteries. In addition to the Gettysburg National Cemetery, the Evergreen Cemetery remains the town's main burial ground; the first ninety-one soldiers from the Battle of Gettysburg were buried there. The ornate gatehouse and home of the caretaker has been mistaken by many photographers as the entrance to the national park and even today remains as one of the most recognized works of architecture associated with the Battle of Gettysburg.

Soldier's National Monument   *Soldier's National Monument*

Water

In the aftermath of the Battle of Gettysburg, water stations returned to normal and soldiers of the Army of the Potomac began the regular process of filling their canteens. The weather had been intensely hot, and during the three-day fight men on the right flank had to draw some of their water from Rock Creek and Spangler's Spring. Soldiers fighting on the left flank dipped into Plum Run, which flowed by the dead animals on Trostle's Farm and passed by Devil's Den and Little Round Top, where the wounded from both sides slacked their thirst in water rich with blood and fecal matter. Because of poor water, dysentery and diarrhea put thousands of soldiers on the sick list, and some of them never recovered. Army water was typically safer than ordinary creek water, but not always, and when soldiers drank water that had not been boiled, they became susceptible to typhoid fever and other disabling and life-threatening diseases resulting from unsanitary field conditions.

Filling Canteens

Filling Canteens

Cooking for the Troops

For more than three weeks, the Army of the Potomac had been constantly on the road, constantly searching for General Robert E. Lee's Army of Northern Virginia. There had never been time to rest, or to just relax under the shade of the trees and enjoy life's comforts. When Lee withdrew from Gettysburg on July 4, the federals were exhausted after three days of fierce fighting. It rained hard for two days, and when fair skies returned, regimental officers joined their collapsible camp tables together for a little libation in the shade of the woods.

A typical officers' mess was run by a sergeant, but most of the cooks and the kitchen squad were African Americans. Some were freemen who joined the army as civilian hands and received wages. Many were ex-slaves who fled from their masters during the war, took refuge in the Union army, and found work as kitchen hands. Many of them were exceptional cooks, having been trained in luxurious southern plantations. They could even make foul-smelling salt beef and pork taste good, which is the reason officers hired them whenever they came into camp looking for work.

Officer's Mess

Officer's Mess

ARMY CAMPS AFTER THE BATTLE

Soon after the battle of Gettysburg, people from nearby towns converged on the town, some to aid the wounded and others to aid the living. Among the sightseers came those looking for work, including laundresses, cooks, nurses, and army wives with children who had been left behind. President Lincoln expected General Meade to follow up on his victory, pursue the Confederate army, and crush it. When Meade expressed satisfaction over repelling Lee's army from Pennsylvania, Lincoln groaned, "Is that all. Will our Generals never get that idea out of their heads? The whole country is our soil."

It was after Meade's refusal to advance that people from all over the country came to take sketch pictures of the battlefield and take photographs of the living and of the rotting carcasses of the still unburied dead. Army camps once again became social centers, and those who were willing to sell their services in exchange for a few coins found plenty of work. Soldiers who had not changed their clothing for more than a week now had help, and for a while laundresses and seamstresses were more popular than whiskey and tobacco.

Tent life

Tent life

Three Captured Confederates

During the Battle of Gettysburg, 5,365 Yankees and 5,425 Rebels went missing. Many of them surrendered, disappeared from their units, and became prisoners of war. Some were captured in battle, some were taken as stragglers, and some were simply tired of fighting, shoeless, and hungry. The three captured Confederates in the stereograph were probably stragglers or deserters because they still carried all their gear and appeared to be alone. They were probably friends serving in the same Confederate company. Had they been captured as part of a regimental unit, there would have been scores of prisoners rather than three.

Many northerners visiting the South became swept into the Confederate Army by conscription as soon as the war began, and the three pictured may have been reluctant Rebels looking for the first opportunity to desert. That opportunity came when an army suddenly moved at night, as Lee's forces did late on July 4. Thousands of Confederate prisoners taken into northern prisons during the war eventually took the oath of allegiance and again became United States citizens while war continued to rage in the South. Perhaps all three men had that in mind when they surrendered.